MARY HUDSON

SMART BOMBS

Tearing Down Strongholds with the Explosive Word of God

SMART BOMBS:
Tearing down strongholds
with the explosive word of God

ISBN-10: 0-615-28381-0
ISBN-13: 978-0-615-28381-4

1st printing, March 2009

2nd printing, July 2012

TABLE OF CONTENTS

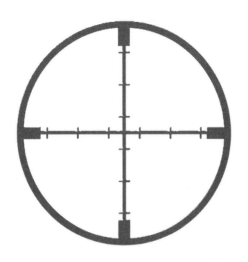

PREFACE

One word from God can crack long delayed destiny in you life. You can re-write your future by an anointed word. God has given you the tongue as a pen of a ready writer. But it is just like taking a photograph. You have to have get that film developed. (Nowadays you just have to download it to your computer.) But the point is, it is not enough just to have a word. You must apply it, vigorously and passionately, if you want vigorous and passionate results. Positive or negative patterns form in your brain after repeating an action time and time again. They are what we call ruts or even strongholds. But ruts can be undone by a word from God's heart. This kind of word has resurrection power in it to demolish long held destructive thought patterns.

A prophetic word can make the river turn in your life from past failure to future victory, from old wounds to healed hearts. When you receive a word from God, how are you going to take it? What should you do with it? What if it doesn't bear witness with your spirit?

"Is not My word like a fire that consumes all that cannot endure the test? Says the Lord, and like a hammer that breaks in pieces the rock of most stubborn resistance?" Jer 23.29 amp

The key is to speak, pray, meditate or mutter the Word. Many people today are "meditating," but they don't know what they are saying. Not so with scripture. You are declaring the word that is eternal and never fades away. God's word in your mouth can destroy the most obstinate problem. You might have stood against some bad habit or attitude all your life but you finally realize you can't do it on your own.

You are not defensively muttering an unknown mantra, but you are taking the offense and destroying the strongholds that have stood against you all your life. The Lord is walking by your side waiting for you to ask Him to help you.

Mt 4.4. says "man shall not live by bread alone but by every word that proceeds out of God's mouth...." If you've been trying to live by what you eat and you have been starving spiritually, you need to change your diet. You have to start feeding your spirit with the same diligence. After all, if you feed your body three times a day and your spirit only once a week at church, no wonder you can't get the victory. Jesus told Martha it was Mary who was seeking the thing that would last forever, as Mary sat at his feet and heard the word.

When you read the word, read it out loud. Faith comes by hearing, and hearing by that word. The most spiritual people you will find, the most victorious, are those who meditate that word and speak it. The Hebrew word for meditation comes from the word hagah, which means to mutter. You need to speak that word to yourself, as the Holy Ghost quickens you, you must release smart bombs of that word against the situation you are facing. Joshua had great success and prospered when he meditated, or muttered the word to himself, day and night. The more consistent you are in doing this, the faster and better your results will be.

There are thousands of thoughts that going through your heads daily. But when you start replacing them with God's thoughts, you enter a whole new realm. Start using smart bombs of His Word as offensive weapons to destroy strongholds in your life and the lives of others. You will make quick work of the battle in front of you. The Centurion knew

Jesus had a smart bomb in His mouth... in Mt 8.8 He knew the authority of Jesus' words. And His words in our mouth are just as powerful as His words in His mouth, as the Lord told Reinhardt Bonnke in a vision one day. Some of you might say, 'Well, what about Job, he said a lot of negative things about God.' However many of the words Job spoke were definitely duds. He did make true statements, but what he said was not the truth.

Negative words almost destroyed him. He opened the door to fear nearly every time he spoke two-thirds the way through the book. In the very first chapter, he set the stage for losing everything by opening the door to fear with his mouth..."For it may be that my sons have sinned and cursed or disowned God in their hearts..."Job 1.5 His sons had not done anything wrong, but just in case they did in the future, Job thought he had better atone for their sins in advance. This is similar to people who have cancer in their family and get the body part removed just in case it shows up later!

The Lord had to allow the enemy to attack Job because he had opened a door with his mouth. What we allow on earth must be allowed in heaven "Whatever you permit or declare lawful on earth must be what is already permitted in heaven." Mt 18.18 He lost his children, possessions, and almost his health because of fear. And he was the richest man in the East! He readily admitted fear was his problem when he said, "for the thing which I greatly fear comes upon me, and that of which I am afraid befalls me." Job 3.25 amp He was afraid of circumstances more than he was afraid of God. We need to be aware of what we are saying at all times. Your life is determined by what comes out of your mouth two inches below your nose. You are the total of your talking yesterday, and Job is a vivid example.

His friend Elihu finally got tired of Job whining and blaming God. He rebuked him and told him to get his words straight, "Job speaks without knowledge and his words are without wisdom and insight." Job 34.35 We can believe God with smart bombs of revelation coming out of our mouth or we can stay negative and just release duds of doubt, which accomplish nothing and make the situation worse. Some peoples' words are so profound, the world sits up and take notice. The famous commercial said it all, "when EF Hutton speaks, everybody listens." So make sure your words are worth listening to.

God spoke and the world was brought into existence. When you as His child speak His word, people are saved, healed and delivered. This cannot be you speaking if you want it to have results, it must be the anointing on you. Otherwise it is just head knowledge, and not from your heart. If you want it to destroy the works of the enemy you had better have the anointing of the Lord on your mouth. Trying to do it in your own strength only brings a mess. Start delivering your words in a small place, a Bible study, to someone you can see the Lord quickening to you. Start blooming where you are planted, start small like Ruth did, gleaning in the corners and continue to seek Him for direction. He will take you right into the center of the field with your Kinsman Redeemer waiting for you.

What you say must line up with God's Word to be effective. Job drew the "worthless conclusion that the righteous have no more advantage than the wicked." Job 35:16 amp If you were to watch television news long enough you might draw that conclusion too. In this last hour it is very important what you put in front of your eyes, since this will determine what comes out of your mouth. Will it be full of faith and power or fear and pity?

"The voice of the Lord makes the hinds bring forth their young, and His voice strips bare the forest, while in His temple everyone is saying, Glory!" Ps 29:9 amp

DEDICATION

Thank you Holy Spirit for breathing on this word, that many people will read it and get a fresh revelation of God's Word, as it applies to their lives personally. Also to my husband Keith, a man who "continues to speak the word of God with freedom and boldness and courage," (Acts 4:31 amp,) and throws out smart bombs regularly; to our three children Angela, Katy and David, whom I speak the following over; "David will say, "I am the Lord's; Angela will call herself by the name of Jacob; and Katy will write (even brand or tattoo) upon her hand, I am the Lord's, and surname herself by the honorable name of Israel." Is 44:5 amp.

We also thank the many prayer warriors who prayed this project through. And niece Jennifer Noble Baumann who helped edit and whose "tongue the pen of the ready writer." Ps 45:1

"Who is like Me? Let him (stand and) proclaim it, declare it, and set (his proofs) in order before Me, since I made and established the people of antiquity. (Who has announced from of old) the things that are coming? THEN LET THEM DECLARE YET FUTURE THINGS." Is 44:7 amp

FORWARD

This book was created from a prophetic word. One word from Him can change your life, and this prophecy from Pastor Gary Greenwald, Irvine, California did just that. "Mary, we were listening to your words and transcribing them, and the Lord showed me that your prophetic is going to take on a new dimension now; you are going to have words that become smart bombs against strongholds in peoples' lives. You are going to direct those words to diseases and strongholds of drug addiction and every kind of demonic thing that has held people captive and you will start speaking to them. Your words will take on a new dimension. They will be piercing. You know when we went to war with Iraq, they were sending those scud missiles, they didn't know where they would hit, Iraq just shot them out there and hoped they would hit something. But America came on the scene and we shot smart bombs. They were laser-guided and they went right to the target. The Lord showed me she is going to start prophesying, speaking smart bombs and people are going to be delivered and set free...."

A prophecy is for whosoever will, so if any of the above strikes a cord in your spirit, take it for yourself and run with it. As a matter of fact, do the same with this whole book. It is written with you in mind.

Chapter 1
"What Is A Smart Bomb?"

Have you ever felt like you were wandering aimlessly on a sea of flotsam and jetsam? That you needed direction and you needed it now? God deals in specifics, He wrote the book of Numbers, He gave the measurements of Solomon's temple, He defined the limits of the sun, the moon, the stars, the earth and even the oceans' tides. He can direct your footsteps daily if you have an ear to hear. In our family of five, two of us are "directionally challenged." The other three love to read and study maps and figure out where we are going and how to get there. But the first two will drive to Los Angeles, CA, and end up a hundred miles down the road in San Diego before they realize they overshot the mark.

If you have ever continued to miss the mark in life, it is time to reposition yourself by hitting the bulls-eye. God shows you how to do that daily with a life giving word from His word. He will also use a prophetic word through an anointed man and woman. But a word through a man's mouth is not as direct as a word straight out of the Bible. Prophecy is second best to the scripture itself. However, a true word from God, whether scripture or prophecy, will bring water to you in a desert, life when death surrounds you and peace in the midst of turmoil. It is like the early rain that cracks dry ground and brings hope to your heart. Many people attend church without even bringing their Bibles today. The Word of God has been devalued, watered down and even dismissed in some congregations for the word of a man. But Jesus says His word is the "same yesterday, today and forever." (Heb 13:8) It is never going to change. It is the one north star in your life you can always count on to show you true direction for your life. Everything and everyone around you might be in a state of flux, but you can go to the bank with God's word when it is firmly embedded in your heart. It will guide you out of your current circumstance, it will show you where His grace and favor is waiting to take you, this word will demonstrate to you that He is always there for you and never leaves you or forsakes you. In this "whatever..." world, we must have a "true north" in our lives by relying on the unchanging Word or we can easily be led astray. With the plumb line established, you can build your life on a secure foundation, a word from the One who gave you your life, the Life-Giver, the Creator Himself. Once it is securely embedded in your heart, you can aim it like a smart bomb into your circumstances. As you roll this sword of the spirit, meditating it over and over in your mind, it becomes an offensive weapon against the strongholds of the enemy.

What is a smart bomb in the natural, anyways?

Regular Bombs

Regular bombs have a sturdy round case filled with explosive material and a fuse mechanism. The fuse has a triggering device or a target–proximity sensor which will set the bomb off. When the device detonates, the fuse ignites material which results in an explosion. The extreme pressure and flying debris of the explosion destroys surrounding structures. This is considered a dumb bomb because it hits the ground without actively steering itself. A plane might have to drop dozens or even hundreds of dumb bombs to effectively take out a target.

However Smart Bombs Are Just The Opposite!

They control their fall precisely to hit a designated target dead on. These munitions are kitted with extra bells and whistles which make them the precise instruments they are. A basic smart bomb will have an electronic sensor system built-in (actually an on-board computer), a set of adjustable flight fins and a battery. This bomb is dropped from a high-speed plane and becomes, really, a very heavy glider. It has forward velocity from the plane, and fins that generate lift and stabilize its flight path. The sensor system itself actually "sees' the target. Old sensors had a problem with cloud cover that could obscure a target.

But the latest and greatest smart bombs aren't bothered by the weather because they use GPS systems like you use in your car. The internal receiver figures out its position by interpreting satellite signals while its guidance system tracks the bomb's movements from its launch position. These precision-guided weapons are self- guiding missiles intended to maximize damage to the target while minimizing the surrounding damage. Bombs used in Iraq were guided by our GPS system.

Scientists are even developing smart bombs for cancer. In Germany doctors are using molecular smart bombs that only explode poison when they hit a tumor and don't harm surrounding tissue.

Smart Bombs Defined Spiritually

A spiritual smart bomb is a rhema word from the Bible or a prophetic word that explodes truth into your heart. This is a word that vibrates in you so strongly you know it is God speaking to you. This word can redirect your future decisions, give you hope when all hope is gone, and bring healing to your heart and mind.

Arkansas Biology teacher Alan Peake was diagnosed with fatal lymphoma, made worse by the fact that his sister had died from it several years before. However, a prophetic word the Lord gave him in one of our meetings brought him the courage to fight through. Two months before he was even diagnosed, a prophetic word declared, "you will be totally healed by the end of the year." An odd word for someone who wasn't even sick at the time! But, if prophecy doesn't line up with your spirit, you just put it on the shelf until it comes to pass or fades away. If it be not of God, it will come to naught. But if He is in it, He will confirm it with signs following. The Lord knows the future, and He knew Alan was going to need this bomb to win the battle.

Doctors may give you a physical report about your body, and they may have the greatest facts in the world to back them up. But the Lord has the truth in Is 53:4-5 with "By His stripes your were healed." It comes down to whose report will you believe, you will make it if you will believe the report of the Lord.

The prophecy gave this science teacher, whose knowledge of the the Lord and His word, the ability to rise above what the doctors were telling him. There was no doubt he could plainly read the reports confirming the cancer, and could feel it with his five physical senses.

But the supernatural truth (which is higher than natural truth!) in his prophecy gave him the courage to fight through impossible odds. Doctors finally told him nothing else could be done, that he needed to go home and put his affairs in order. However Alan was not settling for their report. The triggering device of the prophecy continued to give him hope when there was none. It exploded barriers built up in his mind. A quickened word like this shatters preconceived ideas and blasts you into whole new possibilities for your life. The word God gives you personally will not have the life- changing effect on others' lives as it does on yours. This is God talking to YOU.

So Alan got on the offense with his word after that report, stood out in his back yard, and spoke it out to the Lord, saying, "God, you gave me a word that I would be healed by the end of the year, but the doctors are telling me my time on earth is up! Lord I am taking you at your word...."

The very next day Alan's white blood cell count started to change. By December he was totally cancer-free. Alan was not going to settle for an early eternity. He knew his life here on earth was not done. But Alan had a part to play. He had to get on the offensive with the prophetic word. He had to speak it, pray it out to the Lord. And God healed him! Sometimes we are prideful like Naaman, the general who said he was too good to dip into the muddy Jordan to get healed of leprosy. But his servants reminded him that if the prophet Elisha had told him to do it, he would have obeyed. Naaman humbled himself and got wet, muddy and healed!

Consider Saul on the road to Damascus...He was the only one who actually saw the Lord while the men with him could only sense His presence.

In Acts 8:3 amp Paul "shamefully treated and laid waste the church continuously (with cruelty and violence;) and entering house after house, he dragged out men and women and committed them to prison.."

Then one chapter later in Acts 9:1(amp) Saul is still "drawing his breath hard from threatening and murderous desire against the disciples of the Lord," but at this very moment the Lord calls Saul out of darkness into His marvelous light. "Saul, Saul, why persecutest thou me?"And he said, 'Who art thou, Lord?' And the Lord said "I am Jesus whom thou persecutest: it is hard for thee to kick against the pricks"...And he trembling and astonished, (probably at the fact that the Lord would call him, of all people, and speak to him personally), said, 'Lord, what wilt thou have me to do?' And the Lord said unto Him "Arise and go into the city, and it shall be told thee what thou must do." Acts 9:1-6

Now Saul could have ignored those words and we would not have had two thirds of the New Testament today. But Jesus' words stopped Saul in his tracks.

"Saul, Saul, why persecutest thou me.." had enough anointing on them to make Saul acknowledge Jesus as Lord, turn from darkness to light, even with the blood of Christians still on his hands! Imagine what a word from God can do for you if you are off course even a little bit in your life. You don't have to be a rank sinner to be missing the mark, your sails may just need to be trimmed a few degrees.

Growing up in a city on the California coast, we used to do a lot of sailing. Every time we headed for the offshore islands to scuba dive, we had to be careful to keep the compass at the right longitude and latitude so we would hit the the target, the right island where the water was calm enough to drop anchor.

One or two degrees off, and we could be on our to Hawaii. You might get off course just a couple of notches in your life and it can take you years and thousands of miles to get back on the right track. So consider what an anointed word from the Lord can do to move your life's direction onto the right path.

Never take a rhema or prophetic word lightly word lightly, if it bears witness with your spirit. Transcribe it, carry it with you and pray over it. The Jews carried the word on the little boxes on their foreheads as frontlets.

It was symbolic of the importance of having it on their minds and hearts day and night. But we are talking about not just a word, but the word which confronts you, stops you right where you are. Perhaps you are little off course in life or maybe even heading for destruction. It turns your life around, like it did Saul. Because Saul heeded and obeyed Jesus' Word, he was transformed into another man.

When the Lord gives you an anointed word like this, it is not time to sit back and be passive about it. Get down and pray it through and start acting on the doors He opens for you. When the Lord called us to the mission field, it was as if a finger reached out through the television. A prominent female minister spoke out one day "If you want to do something great for God, go be a minister in France..."

France was not a foreign country for me, I had been going there since I was eleven, as well as attending college in Paris. I traveled there in the nineties with a friend who writes plays for French Christian radio and lives there. Her dramas, resounding with French culture and history wrapped around the Word, struck the heart of the French people.

But a real burden didn't hit on me until this prophetic word was spoken out of the evangelist's mouth. Once the bomb was dropped, however, it was as if the Lord had tattooed the nation on my heart. I was determined to go, this word gave me the courage to get the job done. Doors started opening as we just "happened" to meet a couple who had been having a prayer meeting for France under the auspices of Church On the Way in Van Nuys, CA. They connected us with French pastors for meetings. Our first trip started six months later, and as of this printing we have ministered there nine times in the past five years. Each time the glory over this nation gets stronger, unity among ministry is greater and French people are quicker to acknowledge Jesus as Lord and get filled with the spirit. A recent word for France declared the nation is famous for its fresh bread, beautiful garments, incredible perfume and love. And in the last days this will be its tenor in the spirit, the fresh bread of God's word will be preached everywhere, people will be clothed in robes of righteousness, their prayers will go up as incense to God's nostrils, and the love of God will be prevalent throughout the country.

When the Lord gives you a word, either prophetic or biblical, that rearranges your life, it burns in you. You can't shake it. "Is not My word like fire (that consumes all that cannot endure the test? And like a hammer that breaks in pieces the rock (of the most stubborn resistance?") Jer 23:29 amp This destiny word can change your very existence if you hear the Lord's voice in it.

My husband Keith was born again in the seventies in an apple orchard in Wenatchee, WA. A Bible literally fell open in his hands to the scripture, Romans 10: 9 & 10. A long-haired hippie at the time, he had hitchhiked up to the Pacific Northwest to find a job picking apples. An elderly lady drove by and picked him up in her Volkswagen. After telling him she could only take him a little ways, silence ensued. However minutes later this ordinary looking little old lady burst out into tongues. Even as radical as Keith was, he had never heard anything like this. Then she put her hand on him and continued to pray. Shocked by this action from a senior citizen, Keith sat frozen in the car until she dropped him off on the side of the road. Before he left, however, she handed him the Bible and told him to read it. He threw it into his backpack, never giving it another thought. But carrying sixty pound bags of apples down ladders every day got to be hard work. After a while, Keith was worn out. He could not climb the ladder one more step. He went back to his cabin and cried out, "Lord if You are real, show me!" Dumping out the contents of his backpack onto his bunk, there fell the Bible, staring him in the face. As he took it and examined it, he decided to open it up and read it. After three days of non-stop immersion in the Word, Keith was hooked, and this time it was not drugs. He decided to walk up to the top of a mountain and held the Bible up to the Lord. As he did, the pages fell open to those life-changing words of Romans 10:9 &10, "If thou shalt confess with your mouth and believe in your heart that Jesus is Lord, thou shalt be saved." This scripture exploded all the darkness out of Keith's heart and brought the light of God blasting in. He went back to his cabin and cried for hours. Finally his room-mate came back from work, saw him and was shocked at his appearance. He asked Keith if he was on a bad trip. "No," Keith boldly declared, "I have just found God!" One word from God changed a hardened hippie into a passionate pursuer of His presence.

Another time a pastor and his wife from Columbia, South America, had a prophetic word from God. They prayed over it faithfully for eleven years. The prophecy said they would one day own and live in a beautiful condominium with a view of the city of Cali, in a valley, and would provide hospitality for visiting ministers. The prophecy seemed very remote in their circumstances. But later on, they were praying together and decided it would be wise to buy a house instead of continually paying rent. Another Christian businessman, who owned seven towers of beautiful condominiums in an exclusive gated property with a view and in a valley, offered them the top floor penthouse with owner financing! They were able to move in, and are now able to host visiting ministers. They took God at His word and continued to pray and thank Him for the fulfillment. He was, and always is, faithful to bring His words to pass!

Chapter 2
"The Illuminated Word"

The word illumine means to "enlighten, be luminous, illustrated, to light up or to fire up," according to Webster's' 1828 dictionary. The word of God is a fire that illuminates you. When you are fired up with a personal word from the living God, you are passionate, unstoppable, unbeatable. You are lit up. Circumstances in your life start to flow in the right direction as you allow yourself to be led by this word. You KNOW you are on the right track and it is only a matter of time before the devil bows out of the situation, realizing once again his deception is exposed.

Between the ages of three and fifteen, I had three eye operations on a crossed eye. When you have a turned-in eye, it looks like you have something going on in your body which is much more serious than it really is. In reality your eye just has a lazy muscle. Of course it was very embarrassing to go through elementary, junior high and high school with a turned-in eye. Other kids would bully me, call me retarded, and every other kind of derogatory name they could think of. Every time the date arrived for another operation, I dreaded the thought. The procedure itself was not so bad but doctors had to put what amounted to a "Zorro" eye patch over the recovering eye for three weeks. I looked like a character out of Pirates of the Caribbean.

My self-esteem at such a young age was taking a beating. But I bravely made it through the teasing and name-calling. Finally my mother found a doctor who was world renowned for his corrective eye surgery, and I came out of it at sixteen with straight eyes. However, twenty years later, after being born again, married, with two children, and traveling in ministry with my husband, the eye muscle once again weakened and turned in. What now Lord?

We were evangelists, and there I was, up in front of churches, laying hands on the sick, looking like I needed hands laid on myself. One year we attended a healing and miracle conference with Brother Norvel Hayes, an internationally known healing minister. At an opportune moment I was able to approach him and ask, "I have been confessing the word, Brother Norvel, but this eye is not getting any better, what do I do now?"

"Speak the Word only," was his short but sweet reply. My mind was in turmoil, screaming to my spirit, 'Look at this eye!! Look at these symptoms!! What is this man talking about?' But my heart argued back, 'Agree with the word from the man of God.'

The Lord was gently trying to tell me to take my eyes off myself and look to Him.

So much of the time we have been head taught at the expense of our heart. So many years of education, at least twelve through high school, four more in college, and God help you if you have attended graduate, law or medical school! Your mind is so saturated with head knowledge, but your heart is crying out for truth. There is nothing wrong with head knowledge, but the Word and the Spirit must agree. When a surgeon is a born again Christian, filled with the Holy Ghost, I would much rather have his hands, that are spirit- led, operating on my body than one who is not a believer. His heart would yield to the spirit of God as well as to what he knew by the book.

When you are so immersed in head knowledge, it is as if reason tries to take over your mind. 'This doesn't make sense; how can the word of God in the Bible or a word of prophecy through man alter my body or my destiny?' You become like a doubting Thomas with so much logic and reasoning dominating your heart, you are insisting on seeing it before you are going to believe it. There is nothing wrong with logic or reasoning, but just put the Holy Spirit in the mix. It is so important to have a specific, fired-up word of God to thaw out your heart and bring you out of sterile thinking.

After traveling for nine months in a fifth wheel trailer around the country with our two small children, we settled down in Tulsa, Oklahoma, and based our ministry there.

A born again Jewish evangelist belonged to the church wen attended. He looked at my eye, I told him I was believing God for healing. The Lord quickened a specific word to him for me to stand on. Proverbs 20:12 hit the bulls-eye for this weak eye muscle. 'The hearing ear, the seeing eye, God has made even both of them.....'' God had given me a smart bomb! An even pair of eyes was exactly what I needed. Rather than reverting to my post- operation pirate role again, I knew this time God had other ways of healing me besides a surgeon's knife. He created the world with His words: strengthening an eye muscle was easy. It is just our unbelief that gets in the way. Even as healing in any part of your body is part of God's salvation covenant with you, if you hold onto it.

Dodie Osteen, mother of Joel Osteen, who now pastors the largest church in America, is living proof of that. Diagnosed with metastatic liver cancer over twenty- five years ago, she was given six weeks to live. But Dodie went to war with the word. Confessing healing scriptures at least twice a day, she talks about the battle plan the Lord gave her for healing in her book, <u>Healed of Cancer</u>. She knew she had to not only speak the word but to actually act like she was a healed woman. That was nearly three decades ago, and she is still sitting on the front row of her son's church very Sunday. And still confessing healing scriptures daily.

We become born again through the revelation of Romans 10:9 & 10. "If thou saved...". How much more can we possess the full weight of salvation, which includes healing for our body, through confessing and believing?

So I took ownership of Proverbs 20:12 and started speaking it out loud on a regular basis. For a year and a half, perhaps not as diligently as I should, I would steadily speak that word out my mouth.

Then, one day, we were asked to hold a miracle crusade in Monterrey, Mexico. The very first night a woman with a withered arm was healed, after announcing Luke 6:8-10 to the crowd. ..."And He said to the man with the withered hand, Come and stand here in the midst. And he arose and stood there. Then Jesus said to them, I ask you, is it lawful and right on the Sabbath to do good (so that someone derives advantage from it) or to do evil, to save a life (and make a soul safe) or to destroy it? Then He glanced around at them all and said to the man, Stretch out your hand! And he did so, and his hand was fully restored like the other one." We always believe for miraculous healings to confirm the Word that is preached, and for great breakthroughs to follow the things we do to serve Him. The meeting had a great response, many people were set free. An optometrist in the congregation offered both Keith and I glasses and contacts for better reading.

Contacts! No way was I going to put a piece of plastic film into my eyes... However my husband gently encouraged me that this could be a blessing. Little did I know how much of a blessing he meant, and at the time, he didn't either. So, after suffering for the first couple of hours with these miniature pieces of Saran wrap clinging to my eyeballs, I settled down and allowed the lenses improve my vision.

The next day on the plane home, not only was I seeing better, but my weak eye was correcting by itself. By the time we attended church on Sunday, both eyes were straight!! God had done a miracle through the smart bomb of His word.. I didn't have to go to a Doctor for surgery, just to God's Word and the optometrist He picked as I believed him. This rhema word gave me a miracle in the form of a strong eye muscle, that worked evenly with the other one. We later learned that, in some cases, a contact lens can correct a crossed eye. However, only the Holy Spirit could have known that and gotten me to put it into my eye. After so many years of eye surgery, I would have a real fear come on me when anything tried to come near my eye, much less a contact lens that was supposed to stay there.

And twenty years later I still enjoy the benefits of two perfectly even eyes.

Getting Bold With Your Bomb

The word of God will light up your path. It will illuminate you from the inside out. It is a lamp to your spirit man, leading and guiding you in the right direction.

We cannot be passive about words, it is time to pray for a spirit of boldness. The gifts of the Spirit need to be released throughout the church once again. David ran after Goliath with his mouth open, saying "who is this uncircumcised Philistine who comes against he armies of the living God?' And the Goliath of a problem that stands in front of you is no big deal when you are going after it with a quickened Word of God. Fear always likes to stop you in your tracks and make it a huge deal, but it is up to you to back it down and say no, I am not going to receive a spirit of fear.

Paul, who wrote two thirds of the New Testament, prayed three times for boldness. If it was good enough for him to ask all his followers to pray for boldness, it is important for you to do the same. I have missed it several times by not responding to God when the Holy Ghost drops a word in my heart for someone or for the congregation. Not responding to the Holy Spirit grieves Him, the last thing you want to do.

Let The Light In

Before Saul became Paul, he was the murderous, bloodthirsty Pharisee, destroying every semblance of a Christian that crossed his path. However, once the blinding light of God's glory struck Saul's eyes, he was groveling on the ground for mercy from the One he had so mercilessly persecuted. The Lord stopped him in his tracks with the words, 'Saul, Saul, why persecutest thou me?' Acts 9:4 It was Saul's day of reckoning. As you read along in the word, searching for answers in your daily life, God can give you a kairos moment that changes your whole being. One minute you may not understand why people treated you like they did and the next minute He reveals to you that you are not fighting flesh and blood, but powers, principalities and rulers of this darkness. Saul didn't want to change into another man, but once he heard the word of God uttered out of the Lord's mouth, he was quickly brought to his knees by this divine encounter. Those glorious words changed a fool into a wise man, a wicked man into a righteous one. Of course, Saul had to acknowledge Jesus as Lord with his own mouth before the bomb of God's word was going to crack open a new life for this Pharisee. But once he surrendered, Saul became Paul and the rest is history. He produced the world's greatest selling book, the Bible. All because of six words illuminated by the Holy Spirit to a mass murderer. If just a few simple words can do that to a bloodthirsty religious bigot, what can they do to you, especially if you already know the Lord?

The Lord plainly says in the first chapter of John that he came to bring light into this world. So many people today go looking for a word from God, but fail to go to the source. A prophetic word a man is fine, but it is not the unadulterated word of the living God. When you get a word of direction or healing, wisdom from the Bible points you directly to the answer if you will look hard enough. You will know it is the right word, because it brings peace to your heart. When you get a prophetic word from man, make sure it is of the Spirit, and not like Sister Susie who stood up in a service one day and 'prophesied,' 'As far as I can see God is not mad at thee today....''

A true prophetic word will be backed up by scripture as well as a clear witness in your heart. Or it can be a scripture by itself that lights up your spirit as you read it. Never forget that God is the author of simplicity. However, when things start getting complicated, the water is muddied, you can't find your way and it seems as though you are going deeper and deeper into the swamp, go back to the source. Open the word and ask God for His word for your specific situation. He will never disappoint you. His word will line up with something you are going through. It will be as obvious as the letters on a neon sign. He is NOT the author of confusion, but there is one who is. Lucifer, whose name means light-bearer, is a created being. God created him to be the lead worshipping angel in heaven until he rebelled and took one third of the angels with him. At that point he became the arch-enemy Satan and his angels became demons. But his power will never be greater than God's, and he knows his eventual destiny is the Lake of Fire. But Satan wants the world to believe he is not even real. That is why Americans "celebrate" Halloween every year, they think it is just another holiday. It is a holiday all right, one where more satanic rituals and killings are performed world wide than any other night of the year. He is a defeated foe but an expert deceiver and counterfeiter. Imagine thieves who spend months perfecting the counterfeit hundred-dollar bill. The devil has spent thousands of years perfecting the deception of mankind. But an anointed word is exactly how you sharpen the sword of the spirit and cut him to ribbons in the first place. You have to have a true word from Him. And once you have it, you have to use it by speaking it. with authority. Address the devil with the word. The Bible plainly says when you resist him, he WILL flee. But you can't resist him with fleshly means, it has to be by the spirit. Because the devil is a spirit, the Spirit of Truth will always dissolve his lies and deception if properly and consistently applied.

Many times people are so close to a victory, and that is why the word why the word says "Don't grow weary in well doing. You WILL reap if you faint not." The prophet who spoke to the king illustrates this so well. In essence he said, you have struck two to three times. But, if you will strike five to six times you will have the victory. Keep on going! Don't give up now, you are so close and the enemy is trying to tell you it is no use. But you are always right next to a break through, especially when he is trying to discourage you like that. It is always darkest RIGHT before the dawn. There is true and false light....Jesus is the light of the world...but the enemy comes in as an angel of light. God the father is eternal light: the devil can only deceive with reflected light. So take your authority as a Christian in these last days and use the word to fullest advantage. So many have tried to substitute self- help guides, watered-down messages, seeker-friendly services and making light of the enemy. But the devil is real and he is the author of anything that tries to kill steal and destroy from your life. God has come to counteract his moves and give you abundant life. But it is not going to be handed to you on a silver platter, you will have to go after it with a word that works.

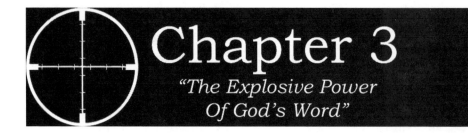

Chapter 3
"The Explosive Power Of God's Word"

When Romans 1:16-17 says "For I am not ashamed of the gospel of Christ, for it is the power of God unto salvation to every one that believeth....for therein is the righteousness of God revealed from faith to faith:", we need to look again at the phrase, "the power of God unto salvation."

The Johnson translation puts it this way: "I am confident that the good news will release God's dynamic energy, which makes all persons whole..."

And the Way translation says: "God's gift of righteousness is revealed in it, (the gospel) lifting men from one step of faith to another..."

The Phillips translation reads, "I have witnessed its divine power to free men from the bondage of sin..."The resurrection power in God's word is unlike anything on earth.

If a person could just get a glimpse in his heart of the dynamic energy involved here, the Bible would be closer to him than any cell phone or ipod ever could be. Consider, if you are saved, how the word in the prayer of salvation took a split second to change your mind, your will and your emotions, literally everything that operates in your soul, how your wants and desires started to change as the Word washed like a waterfall over your heart. How, for the first time in your life, you could actually understand what the Bible was saying because your spirit was alive unto God, the Master and Lord of all spirits.

Finally He had a line of communication with you! Electricity has to have a conduit to run on, and the Spirit of God has to have a heart alive unto Him to reveal His word to. The Lord will drop an illuminated word into your heart at the most unexpected times. He does not want you to have everything figured out. Leave room for the Holy Spirit to do "Abundantly above all you dare ask or think..." Eph 3:20 He wants you to trust Him with simple childlike faith. You say, 'you must be kidding, Mary, I have had twelve years of high school, four years of college,' (or maybe you even have a masters, doctors, lawyers or nursing degree.) You say 'I have too much knowledge just to do something so simplistic as trust God.' That is right. You have been head taught at the expense of your heart. Your spirit is starving for spiritual truth while your mind is full of book learning. But it is God's truth that keeps you balanced with all the facts and figures you cram into your mind for exams, gives you the favor to be at the right place at the right time, the wisdom to know how to handle the skills you have spent so many years learning. Always put His wisdom before the world's wisdom first and you will stay true to His purpose for your life. That is what you did with when you asked Him into your heart. When you go through school, it takes nine months to graduate to the next grade. Natural learning is a gradual process. But when the light of God's word strikes your heart, you are ready to accept salvation in an instant. Preconceived ideas drop off your mind like mold dissolving when bleach hits it. That's what the word "quickening" really means.

When God "quickens" His word to you, that word, like music, bypasses your brain and lights up your heart. Now, as we said earlier, the enlightened word you get from the Bible is pure and untouched by man. The prophetic word from man is good, it is divinely inspired but it is filtered through the human personality. It is not straight from the source. The difference is sort of like spring water and water purified by reverse osmosis. The prophetic word from man is filtered through the human personality. Not only is the prophetic word second best, you have to check with your spirit to see if what is said is God, or if the person prophesying is operating out of a familiar spirit. If it is the Lord, it will be edifying, uplifting and comforting. If not, it will be judgmental and condemning.

The Bible talks about the different ways the Lord can drop His word into your heart. Of course as we said, the written word becoming a life-giving rhema word to you is His number one way of speaking to you. But a prophetic word or gesture can also come to you in many different ways. My husband was taking his clothes to the cleaners one morning after coming home from a meeting. We lived in an area of Southern California that had had a glut of home building since the year two thousand. As he was driving down the road by a new subdivision, a huge white vinyl sign on the fence caught his eye. The words read, "Final Phase Has Been released..." While this would have been an ordinary message in most developments, Keith knew the Lord was saying to him, 'you are living in the last days, son. The final plan for my people has been put in place. My son Jesus is coming back very, very soon.' It was so dramatic that he would preach about this sign and its message for years afterwards.

Prophetic words can come to you, or you can just start speaking what the Lord says to you, and they too can explode strongholds off your mind and heart. When I am in front of people and about to speak a word into their lives, God will show me their next level of ministry or next move in their life. Or he will give me a picture of what is going on in their heart or body. If it lines up with something they are already dealing with, then this word just puts pressure on the situation to release even a little more. When the prophetic word comes to you, you may only receive one or two words, but be faithful to step out over the aching void of faith, speak those words out and watch the Holy Spirit supply the rest. After all you are only doing this as He wills anyways.

If a person is only prophesying from head knowledge, he can easily get over into spiritual manipulation or even charismatic witchcraft, where so-called prophecy is trying to control a person. All prophetic words must line up with the word to demonstrate His truth. Prophecy, tongues and interpretations are only three of the nine spiritual gifts. Most people who operate in one gift or another will have a particular leaning in the direction the Holy Spirit wants to use you in. "But to each one is given the manifestation of the (Holy) Spirit (the evidence, the spiritual illumination of the Spirit) for good and profit." 1 Cor 12:7 amp

Even with children, their gifts are obvious if you observe them long enough. When children become adults, their gifts do not leave them but really develop even more. After all, training up a child in the way he should go, according to his individual gift or bent, does not disappear once they become eighteen. The Lord has given each person a uniqueness in certain areas that are totally different than others. And, it will be clearer and clearer to you as you operate in your gift, that this is what you are supposed to be doing.

When my husband and I were first married, we attended a marriage conference led by Buddy and Pat Harrison, son-in-law and daughter of Kenneth E. Hagin. The Harrisons were well known for their ability to move in spiritual gifts such as tongues and interpretations as a couple. The founders of Harrison House Publishing, Buddy and Pat had written several books on the Holy Spirit.

As we sat in that conference that day, the Lord's voice the Lord's voice spoke clearly to me, saying, "This is how the Holy Spirit will use you for the rest of your lives." He was referring to the spiritual gifts of prophecy, tongues and interpretations that the Lord used the Harrisons in. And that is exactly how we have operated since receiving that word from the Lord.

Receiving a Prophetic Word

As previously mentioned, a true prophecy is for edification, exhortation and comfort. Anything that condemns, disparages or belittles you is not of God. The Holy Spirit will convict you but never condemn you. "For God so LOVED the world, He gave His only begotten son, that whosoever believeth on Him should have eternal life, 17 For God did not send the Son into the world in order to judge (to reject, to condemn, to pass sentence on) the world, but that the world might find salvation and be made safe and sound through Him." John 3:16-17

God is a God of love. It is the love of God that draws men to repentance. A true prophetic word can be like a heavenly bomb that blasts all the hindering spirits out of the way and brings a refreshing wave of hope to your life.

A young man we met while ministering in Oklahoma twenty years ago was playing the organ in a small rural church one Sunday, and we were the guest speakers. A Bible student, he was planning on returning to his native New Jersey after graduation. But God had other plans for Darrell Copes, and needed to give him a heads up. A word came forth that he would travel with a world famous minister, play music and heal the sick. This was a lot for a young, black first year Bible student to swallow. But six months later Darrell was invited to travel on the worship team of one of the leading teachers of the day, and he ministered with this man of God nationally and internationally for nine years afterwards.

How Do You Handle A Bomb Once It Is Dropped?

Gingerly to be sure. If the inspired word is something that lines up with your heart, and you are facing a test, God wants to encourage you to stay strong. He is indicating to you that this word will be the victorious end result if you don't give up. However, if the word you receive does not bear witness to your spirit, just put it on the shelf and leave it alone. If it comes to pass, praise God. If not, you have not wasted any time thinking about it! Also be aware that some words will not come to pass right away. But believing the word and wielding it like a sword at the enemy when you are tempted to quit will quicken the pace. " Jesus saith unto her (Martha),' Said I not unto thee, that, if you would believe, you would see the glory of God?'" John 11:40

When you aim a word, at a problem that would have taken you twenty-five years to solve, that anointed word can shrink the situation to one year, one month, one day, one hour or a flat-out suddenly. Think about it, When God spoke His word in Genesis one, He created planets and universes with His mouth. When God speaks His word, His word actually creates what He speaks. You, in the image of God, can speak an impregnated word, a word full of His spirit, and it will become what you say if you will continue to believe Him and say it long enough. "SAY unto this mountain, be thou removed..." Mark 11:23. David ran after Goliath with his mouth open. He told the Israeli soldiers around him, "Who is this uncircumcised Philistine that he should defy the armies of the living God?" 1 Sam 17:26 amp. Then, after David made that bold declaration of faith, he did not wait for doubt to set into his heart, he went after the giant's head. He knew if he thought about the size of his enemy for any amount of time, he would lose heart and faint. But David made a courageous statement in the face of impossible odds and took action on his words to back them up.

Hebrews 11 is the hall of faith chapter. It talks about heroes of faith who were "prompted, actuated by faith..." vrs 4, "urged on by faith", vrs 8, "because of faith" vrs 11, "with eyes of faith" vrs 20, "aroused by faith" vrs 24, "motivated by faith" vrs 27, and "by the help of faith" vrs 33. These Biblical giants did not just say they were going to do something, when God spoke to their hearts, they got moving. Procrastination is a dream killer. You might have a lot of visions about what God wants to do with your life, but what are you doing to actually make it come to pass? David made his faith a reality when he acted on his words, when he did something about what he said.

God can provide for you in the most unusual ways if you will just trust Him. He can be very creative in His provision for you. In 1 Ki 17: 1-9, the prophet Elijah was so disgusted with the current culture of paganism in the land, he declared a drought. Consequently even Elijah had nothing to eat or drink himself. But "the word of the Lord came to him, saying, go from there and turn east and hide yourself by the brook Cherith, east of the Jordan. You shall drink of the brook, and I have commanded the ravens to feed you there." Elijah obeyed God's word and was sustained for a time. What is interesting is that it was obviously a word from the Lord. Ravens are very selfish birds. Like vultures, they prey on carcasses and keep everything for themselves. For these birds to bring sustenance to anyone besides themselves is a miracle in itself! When Elijah obeyed God's voice, the birds obeyed their Creator and fed him. So when the brook dried up, Elijah heard God's voice again and was ready to obey it with even more zeal. But this time the Lord told him to go to a most unlikely source of supply. An impoverished widow and her son had decided to bake their last loaf of bread and die.

But vrs 9 says this is exactly where the Lord wanted Elijah to be! "Arise, go to Zarephath, ..and dwell there. Behold, I have commanded a widow there to provide for you..." Elijah proceeds to ask this hungry woman for a piece of her last loaf, what nerve! No, on the contrary, the Lord was providing a way of escape from certain starvation for this family. Giving was their only way out of famine. God sent Elijah to this widow not so he could get something to eat, but so this widow and her son would live and not die. Elijah was prompt to give the word, and the widow explained to the prophet this was all she and her son had to eat instead of give. But the famous words out of his mouth gave her the courage to obey, "Fear not." Fear will always stand in the way of your faith. Bold words declared under the unction of the Holy Ghost will sweep fear away, followed up by bold action every time.

So do not hesitate if you are about to walk out on a faith cliff. Speak the word empowered by the Holy Spirit and the Lord will sustain you. Fear not and keep your eyes on Him and that word. And continue to rejoice, for your praises form a highway for Him to bring your answer down. "Sing to God, sing praises to His name, cast up a highway for Him who rides through the deserts – His name is the Lord – be in high spirits and glory before Him!" Ps 68:4

Chapter 4
"Discerning A Smart Bomb"

He holds everything together by the Word of His power. A photon is a particle of light that is like God, it is omnipresent, everywhere at the same time. The Bible says it is literally God's Presence that holds everything together. Scientists have theories but do not really understand gravity, the force that causes everything to fall to earth, until you reach a certain point in the atmosphere where an object goes into free fall in space.

The word of God is alive; it is full of His presence. One word from Him can address you right where you are and bring momentum where there was stalemate. His personal word lighting up your heart when you read it can bring the solution you are so desperately searching for. God knows what you are going through, and there is nothing the Word doesn't cover about your problem. His word can frame and rearrange your mind and the situation you are facing.

A word proceeds (moves – goes out of) God's mouth. God created everything. He IS the creator. When He acts, speaks or moves He is creating. Once he creates or frames a word that burns in your heart (He is the night light of your soul!), He is in the process of creating something new in your life...God's word is similar to a personal visitation from the Lord Jesus Christ Himself. But sometimes you need to get still and quiet enough to listen. The Centurion illustrated this when he asked Jesus just to "speak the word only and my servant will be healed." He knew it was vital that he stop at that moment and listen to the Master. You can do the same thing yourself as you speak and declare the words He gives you. So breathe the life of God onto your situation by speaking the Word He whispers in your ear.

The worlds were framed by the word of God. A frame outlines a photograph, it brings it into prominence, it emphasizes what you are looking at. That frame is waiting for you to step into it. The picture will never be completed until you make a move.

His word will clarify and magnify the answers to the problems in your world. Framing a word will give you the practical wisdom to walk into your calling. God is speaking to you. This "frame" outlines the miracle He has for you if you will just act on it.

This word can illuminate the moment and bring peace into a troubled situation. Years ago when I was first born again, I worked as a radio news director at a large country and western radio station in Las Vegas, Nevada. An on-fire Christian, I would witness to anyone that would listen. My superiors were not keen on my zeal however, and did everything they could to squelch my newfound faith. Country and western lyrics often emphasize how "my husband left me for another woman." Not exactly uplifting but the words and bouncy melodies appeal to peoples' emotions, sell advertising and keep the station in business. My news broadcasts at the top of the hour required a strong and confident voice. Often my persecutors would walk into my studio and deliberately throw me emotionally off kilter, often to tears. It would be hard to talk, much less anchor, the news. However a lady minister mentoring me at the time said, "Have a small Bible with you during times like that. Let God speak to you." "After all," she continued, "He has the peace that passes all understanding. Let His peace be your umpire in every situation, the final settling, deciding factor." Col 3:15 amp So the higher-ups would rush into my studio about twenty minutes to the hour, almost every day, to see if they could throw me for a loop. By this time I had gotten my Disc Jockey saved in the cubicle across me, as well as the girl who was the number one Las Vegas TV anchorwoman. She, another fired-up Christian reporter and I would show up and ask questions at celebrity interviews. After the other microphones and cameras were gone, we would believe God to have an opportunity to witness as the Holy Spirit opened the door. Jane Fonda, Willy Nelson, Ronald Reagan (who was already a Christian but glad to hear there were Christian reporters out there), Mohammed Ali and David Frost were a few of the well-known people we were able to pray with.

My tormentors showed up right before airtime. We should just get used to it and laugh back at the devil's tactics, after all, "he who sits in heavens laughs in derision at the enemy..." Ps 2:2. So I quickly learned being defensive in this situation was not going to make the difference. My pastor friend showed me the best defense in the spirit is a great offense – with the word cutting through my feelings, and releasing a victor mentality instead of acting like a victim. And one word from God will do the same thing for you every single time, if you rely on it first and not your friends or the telephone.

Consequently, I started getting tough on my feelings and determined I was not going to burst into tears at every cutting remark. I would open my Bible, God would quicken a scripture, and I would give the devil a mouthful under my breath. It worked for Jesus on the mount of Temptation in Mt 4:4, when the devil dared him to "command these stones to be made loaves of bread", after he had fasted forty days. And the Lord answered, "It has been written, man shall not live by bread alone but by every word that comes forth from the mouth of God." The Word is what we MUST have in these last days. Life-giving words coming out of God's mouth, and His mouth is His Word speaking to you.

During these times, peace would flood my heart and mind. My emotions would calm down and my voice would take on the resilient alto tone it was known for over the Las Vegas airwaves, instead of a shaky vibrato. Only the Lord can bring peace in the middle of such a storm. You can be fighting with your husband and all of a sudden the Word that is planted in your hear begins to speak to you, "A soft answer turns away wrath." Prov 15:1 Your heart logs onto this still small voice and starts to digest it in your spirit. A cow has three stomachs and digest its cud three times. Sometimes that is how we need to meditate the word. Keep chewing on it until it becomes reality for you. You sense yourself starting to calm down as you come under its authority, and you know you are hearing His voice. Consequently the strife ceases and unity starts to restore the relationship.

I always wanted to figure out, HOW is He going to bring peace? It is going to require diligence on our part: Diligence to seek Him until He illuminates that word that will minister to your heart and change your direction in life or even your attitude. Diligence to read it out loud, which can also highlight it, since faith comes by hearing, and hearing by the word of God.

And, once that Word gets illuminated, once you see it, you can't sit there like a spectator at a ball game, you have to take it and use it if you expect it to work for you. Sometimes we will sit and analyze what we are hearing instead of taking action, much to the enemy's delight. Procrastination is a dream killer. One of my favorite scriptures is, "He makes my feet like hinds' feet and will make me to walk (not to stand still in terror, but to walk) and make (spiritual) progress upon my high places o(of trouble, suffering or responsibility)!" Hab 3:19 amp See, the enemy wants to stop you from acting on the Word. He wants to put fear on you to arrest you and your destiny in its tracks. But stand UP to it. If someone came into your house and started hauling away all your furniture, computers, clothes, etc., you wouldn't stand there and the thief to get away with it, would you? Same thing with fear! Tell this spirit to "git" right on down the road, and shred the devil's plan into confetti. But without the Word, fear will just stand there and laugh at you. You have to rise up boldly like every other hero of the Bible and be a lion of the tribe of Judah. You have to come to the realization that the weapons of your warfare are not carnal but mighty through God to the pulling down of strongholds. This humanistic world wants to emphasize everything BUT the Bible, because the devil knows how powerful God's word is. But Christians need to go back to basics.

The enemy is the author of procrastination and would love to see you follow suit. When you hesitate over a word that has been spoken to your heart, the moment to act, to believe, can be lost. It is like when the Holy Spirit created the earth out of an empty waste in Genesis 1:2 amp, 'The Spirit of God was moving (hovering, brooding) over the face of the waters." Even earth that was without form and void that became teeming with life as God spoke life to it. Or how His Holy Spirit hovered over Mary and she became pregnant with Jesus. Even Mary's miracle required her vocal consent, her agreement. "Be it done unto me according to thy Word." Luke 1:38 There is so much power available to you when you agree with His word.

Your miracle will need your voice. The quicker you act on what God is saying, the more easily and dramatically that miracle will occur. And the more determined and expectant your attitude is, the more easily the answer can slide right into your life.

Speak It Out.......

There was a movie once where a king issued a royal decree. He wrote it down, then horseback riders were sent throughout the country, to "declare the decree' to the citizens of that kingdom; like Esther did for King Ahasuerus when he allowed her to revoke the law that would have killed all the Jews in Persia. EST 8:8 -14 or as Caesar Augustus did when he required the whole Roman Empire to be registered, and Joseph and Mary went up to Bethlehem where Jesus was born because of that decree. Luke 2:1-7 The king's decree was not something to trifle with, it was the law of the land and had to be obeyed.

God's word is the His decree for your life, and a specific word will overcome specific situations. When we go forth and declare God's word out of our mouths, when our hearts are full of faith, those faith-filled words establish the life of God in our lives where there has been depression, despair and the death of our dreams.

When the royal decree is pronounced, things begin to change!

You can spend the rest of this year whining about your situation, reveling in being a victim, or you can rise up and take the word and use it against the enemy to be the victor that God created you to be. As one anointed minister friend of mine says, "Christ in you is the hope of glory: help yourself!"

We are the ones who choose our attitudes. Psychologist Victor Frankl was in a Nazi concentration camp during World War II. His famous saying was "They can take anything they want from me, but they cannot take my attitude." Your optimism or pessimism will chart the course of your life, depending which way you steer the boat of your heart. How you think about yourself can cause you to develop your God-given talents or to live off of welfare. And your attitude and success in life is vitally connected to how much time you spend reading and speaking the Word. If you have asked Jesus in your heart, there is no room to fail if you will re-program your mind with the New Testament and Paul's prayers in the epistles instead of The Bachelor or Desperate Housewives on television. Your attitude can be re-programmed with the life of the word. You can reprogram your computer at the touch of a button; your mind and your heart need re-programming too on a daily basis.

A Smart Bomb Brings Clarity

You may have been trying to understand what to do, how to handle a situation, or you may be like Brother Kenneth E. Hagin in the early part of his ministry, where money was scarce and he had to travel hundreds of miles in between meetings to get back to see his family. His bald tires, desperate to be changed, would scream at him as he drove down the country roads "What are you going to do now? What are you going to do now?" He knew he didn't have the fifty dollars it would take in those days to replace a set of tires and didn't see where it was going to come from in the natural. However, those facts did not deter him from the truth. He knew God's word would not fail him. He boldly answered those tormenting thoughts, "I'm going to act like the Bible is true, and believe God." And the money would come in every single time.

Determination and clarity will cut through the fog. Sometimes it seems like you are never going to make it, like your goal is a million miles away. However, if you will just keep declaring and decreeing the clear word that God has given you, what the Doctors say will take six months to heal will turn into three months, then two, then total healing. But football players never win the Super Bowl just by "trying." It is by dogged persistence to win, and to repeat the same basic steps day after day, by playing game after game, starting from the weakest opponents and moving up to the strongest. With every step comes greater clarity and more confidence, you can do this! You can do ALL things through Christ who strengthens you. And your path becomes brighter and brighter with each new step as you slash away at the jungle of circumstances around you with the machete of His Word.

Chapter 5
"Smart Bombs Explode Barriers In Your Life"

God's word will pulverize the biggest stronghold in your life if applied consistently and relentlessly enough. Jesus is simple and His methods are not difficult. "But I fear, lest by any means, as the serpent beguiled Eve through his subtlety, so your minds should be corrupted from the simplicity that is in Christ." 2 Cor 11:3 The enemy is the author of confusion and likes to make people think that psychiatry, psychology, New Age philosophy or ANYTHING besides God's Word is their answer. Jesus is so simple, people think, "I need to get delivered of alcohol, drugs, lust, whatever the stronghold is..." and that may be true. But how you go about getting that deliverance is what makes the difference whether relief is temporary or permanent. Anointed ministers of God can lay hands on you and a demonic spirit will leave you if you are willing to let it go. Or you can simply take the time to read the word for concentrated periods of time, as Psalms says, "How can a young man (or woman) cleanse his way? By taking heed according to Your word." Ps 119:9

Man always tries to complicate God, but He wants us to come with childlike faith. An anointed Word is actually an encounter with God. Otherwise Christianity can become religious, just a dry bones routine. Moses and the Israelites had to rely on fresh manna daily, otherwise it turned stale in their mouth if stored or eaten the next day. The Lord has a fresh word for you every day, He wants you to keep coming back to Him and not rely on man.

Jesus IS the Word, "And the Word became flesh and dwelt among us, and we beheld His glory, the glory as of the only begotten of the Father, full of grace and truth." John 1:14 His word is always talking to you. His resurrection power makes the scripture come alive. But it only speaks to you if your ears are open to hear. God spoke to Paul the apostle but Paul was the only one who heard the Lord's voice. The men with him heard a voice, but they could not hear what that voice was saying. The Lord spoke to Moses but the people couldn't understand what He said unless Moses interpreted it. But we do not need an interpreter nowadays because God has left us His Holy Spirit to speak to us when we read the word.

The power the Word has in your mouth to tear down strongholds is unparalleled. When the Lord told Joshua and Caleb to go and take the promised land, the land was theirs on His authority. But they still had to fight off the squatters! The point was, God was on their side, and they would not fail if they just persevered and enforced their victory. My son David attended Christian school during elementary school but decided to attend a public school for high school. I knew he was not going to hear anything about the Bible in that setting. Every morning he left the house I would say to him, 'David, you are a mighty man of God, a sign and wonder man.' These words did not fall on deaf ears, although he did not respond much at the time. After graduating he told me, 'Mom, you don't know how many times those words you spoke over me every day kept me out of trouble.' Praise God, you might not see the fruit of your confession immediately, but rest assured when you speak the word over your children or any situation it is pushing back the forces of darkness in the unseen realm. The Lord is "far above all power, principality and dominion.." Eph 1:21. This is often more evident in third world countries, when the Word of God, energized by the Spirit of God, is spoken: demon powers retreat. Christians in these countries do not have as many distractions or opportunities as industrialized nations. Aggressive evangelism always pushes back the powers of the air.

But How Do You Stay On Fire To Boldly Evangelize The Nations?

Having the Word of God coming out of your own mouth through prayer, praise, preaching or confession is the best way you can fan the flames. It stirs up the gift within you, keeps you fired up and stops your spirit from sinking within you.

One prophetic missionary prayed throughout the nation of Japan twenty two times, reading the Bible out loud as she rode the train through every town and village. She was, and still is, fired up about what God is doing in this Asian nation. She praises, worships, declares and decrees everywhere she goes throughout the country. Her fire never goes out. Consequently the enemy has backed down there. Christian churches have made notable inroads in Japan through the consistent declaration of God's word, with the help of intercessory prayer warriors like this lady. Manifestations become less frequent and Christians become bolder where the Lord is worshipped and His word is established as the plumb line for a nation. But where He is dishonored, demonic powers start to press in again.

Elijah told the king when he shot three arrows through the window that he was not persistent enough! He said to the King he should have shot them five or six times if he wanted to see victory.

Often your victory is right around the corner, and you are almost to the top when the enemy vigorously discourages you from continuing onto the other side. Sometimes we must be relentless with the Sword of the Spirit, refusing to back down in front of the most obstinate principality. Only clear focus on the Word will enable us to keep going when it feels like we are flying in a fog and cannot see the ground, when we are cruising only on what the plane's instruments tell us. In other words, you are moving out only on what God's word speaks to you personally, and not on circumstances that are screaming "defeat."

Joshua did not attack Jericho on the very first day. Those walls were thick and seemingly impenetrable. He and his army slowly encompassed them for six days, striking fear in the hearts of the inhabitants. And, finally, on the seventh day, after six days of silent marching, he has the priests and all the warriors march around the city seven times in one day, blowing their trumpets. This must have really put the population of the city into fever pitch. The priests were instructed to make one long trumpet blast, and when the people heard that, "then all the people shall shout with a great shout, then the wall of the city shall fall down flat." Joshua 6:5. There was no middle ground in this battle, or any battle. The Lord knew Joshua had to totally defeat his enemy and take no prisoners. You cannot fool around with strongholds in your life. They cannot be coddled or excused away with such reasoning as "that is the way I was born..." No, that is the way the enemy would like to make you think, that you are a victim of circumstances and nothing can ever change that. Fornication, adultery, lasciviousness, uncleanness and homosexuality are all spirits and can be cast out of your spirit, but you have to want to be free. First of all, God is not as interested in your sexuality as He is in your spirituality. Once your spirit lines up with His, everything else comes into order. You have to be willing to be willing. Of course you can ignore deliverance, live a life of compromise and misery and suffer eternal consequences. That is the choice you make here on earth. But why do that when one word from God, one prayer of deliverance can set you totally free? "Whom the Son sets free is free indeed!" John 8:36 God does not do things half way. He wants you to have complete victory in your life.

When your spirit is vitally united to God, and your soul is in communion with His word of victory, the nature of the flesh is dethroned. The soul is deceitfully wicked who can know? That is why you have to wash it with the word on a daily basis. It can go back to being wicked just through neglect. If you don't mop your kitchen floor on a regular basis, the linoleum goes from white to gray to brown to black with everyone's dirt tracked in the house every day. So will your soul crumble under the weight of the world without a constant renewing of your mind in His word.

The Israelites used to put frontlets on their foreheads to remind them to always keep the word of God first and foremost on their minds. They knew in order to win the battles that lay before them in the book of Joshua, they had to fight in His strength as well as under His direction. Jericho was only the first of many battles they would face, even though the Lord had authorized them to take the land. "I sought (inquired of) the Lord and required Him (of necessity and on the authority of His Word), and He heard me, and delivered me from all my fears." Ps 34:4 amp He hears you because of the authority that His word has when you present it to Him.

He wants to communicate to you through His word, His word is Him talking to you, showing you how to walk out of bad situations into a great and glorious future that He has planned for you. The Bible is God's language, the premier way He speaks to you every day. There is the logos, which is the written letter of the law. Then there is the fresh word for you personally today, the rhema word, that you can take to the bank because you know God is speaking to you about your own personal situation. This is the word that quickens your heart when you read it, it is a passage or phrase of scripture imbued with the still small voice of the Lord through it talking directly to you. It is a God-breathed word that destroys strongholds when consistently applied. It is like He is taking the written word, the logos, and breathing life on it, bringing it into your situation right now and making it rhema for your life.

I was seated on a plane for Hawaii with the rest of the passengers, waiting for the aircraft to pull out of its bay at the Los Angeles, California, airport. We were expecting to feel a slight jolt as the plane started to move down the runway, but it just sat there, with all of us in it. After a half an hour of this inertia, the stewardess came over the loudspeaker announcing something was wrong with the electrical system and they were trying to fix it. Another hour later, airplane personnel ushered all of us off the aircraft, declaring it unsafe to fly that night. By that time I was tired. Anxiety started attacking my mind about even getting back on another plane. But all of a sudden the Lord quickened a word to me, "Fear not, (Mary), I am your Shield, your abundant compensation and your reward shall be exceedingly great." Gen 15:1 amp Seeing that scripture filled me with courage and assurance that God was with me, and I was going to get to the islands with no problem. When I stepped on the next plane, my assigned seat was an emergency row exit seat this time, with twice the legroom. It was almost like getting an upgrade. I had the whole row to myself and the rest of the plane was packed. "The blessings of the Lord maketh rich and add no sorrow to it...." Prov 10:22

I was confident we were going safely to the other side, and I was going to be able to lie down and take a nap on those empty seats while we did it. Speak that word out and watch strongholds crumble before your eyes.

When Jacob blessed his sons, the word of his blessing actually changed the inheritance order. There is nothing impossible with God. If the enemy has stolen money, lands or inheritances from you in the past, start to claim it back with the word of His grace. You are a king and priest according to Revelations. Kings make decrees. They go out over all the land and their decrees stand firm. Rise up and be all you are meant to be. Declare and decree your future to the enemy, the Lord and all the angels. The Lord hearkens to His word.

Chapter 6
"Get Bold With The Word"

One Word From God Can Birth Things.....

"The voice of the Lord makes the hinds bring forth their young, and His voice strips bare the forest, while in His temple everyone is saying, Glory!"

Ps 29: 9 God will get your work done for you while you shout and praise and declare His glory. Boldly declare scriptures that are smart bombs in your life out loud. People sometimes call this confessing the word, or a prophetic declaration – however you mash your potatoes, with peels, garlic pods or parmesan cheese, they are still mashed potatoes.

Just Do It, Like Nike Says

No one else is going to speak over your life, family and destiny for you but yourself. "You shall also decide and decree a thing, and it shall be established for you; and the light of God's favor shall shine upon your ways." Job 22:28 amp Your spirit believes your voice before it will believe any other voice.....mainly because it has heard it longer.

"Decree" means to speak it to your peers and the church, but "declare" means to send that word straight into the heavenlies. God says to put Him in remembrance of His Word. After all, He watches over it to perform it.

After All, He Watches Over His Word To Perform It...

Dr. David Yonggi Cho pastors the largest church in the world, 750,000 people. But he did not start out that way. He was a poor pastor in the slums of Seoul, South Korea, with no means of transportation and no place to work on his sermons. One day he prayed and asked God to give him a bicycle so he could visit people in his congregation, and a desk where he could study. For six months he continued to petition God, but the heavens were like brass. Finally he went to the Lord and said, 'God what is the problem here?' The Lord answered him and said, 'Son, there are many bicycles and desks in Seoul. What kind do you want?' So Cho made a specific request for a red Schwinn American-made bicycle, and a desk with a chair he could swivel around in, 'like a big shot.' Some days later an American colonel asked him to come and help load his moving van because he was returning to the States after a tour of duty in Korea. After packing the van to capacity, a bicycle and desk were left that would not fit anywhere on the truck. So the colonel asked Cho if he would like to have these items. Of course the bicycle was a red American made Schwinn, and the desk had the swiveling chair! Naturally Cho was delighted, thanked the colonel and profusely thanked God for such a wonderful answer to his prayer. But he clearly noted that it was only answered when he got bold and specific about what he was praying.

In the same way, the Lord is watching over the Word you speak out of your mouth, the specific word, before He will, or even can, perform it. When you dare to take your place with Jesus, you as a member of the body of Christ have to voluntarily surrender your will to His will and cooperate with Him. He wants you to so identify with Him, the Mighty warrior, and believe His word so strongly that the tenacity of your faith brings life to those words when you speak them. His word gives you a sense of righteousness

when you let it have the central place in your life and your voice. When God's word operates in your life, you have the sword of the Spirit you need - the rhema word the Holy Spirit quickens to your heart. It gives you the peace you need from the attacks of the enemy. "Stand therefore, having your loins girt about with truth," Eph 6:14. The written word of God is the truth you must have in the midst of a battle.

People think it is spiritual to be passive but that is not what God says, "If you abide in Me and My words abide in you, you shall ask what you will, and it shall be done unto you." John 15:7. God is trying to impress you to get up and be bold and ask what you will.

Many believers think a submissive speaking of "Thy will be done" will get the job done. But it won't happen. God has already done all He is going to do for you when He sent Jesus to the cross. Jesus paid the price for everything and has given you the authority to act and speak in his Name. But you have to appropriate these promises and go for it. God uses your spirit and your voice as His agent on earth as long as you are yielded to Him. God is a mighty God, the Lion of the tribe of Judah. If we are created in His image, we are to be equally as courageous and fearless. He wants us to actively enter into His plan instead of passively yielding to circumstances that we actually have authority over, if we will but stand up and speak to the winds and the waves of circumstances.

When you definitely appropriate God's word, it is more than just underlining it in your Bible. You are a speaking spirit that MUST speak God's promises in order to put His life into your life. When you believe God, you enter into rest. You can then praise God that His promises are true. Sarah did just that in Hebrews 11:11 as she was "counting Him faithful who promised...," while she waited to get pregnant at 90 years of age.

The Lord leads us to do a lot of meetings overseas which requires us to take long airplane flights...costing thousands of dollars. One day in an office meeting we were discussing an upcoming Far East trip, and the need to book the airfare as soon as possible. A comment was made that the budget for this had not shown up yet. But something rose up inside of me, and I proclaimed that could change shortly. Within five minutes the phone rang and a partner was on the line saying they were sending more than enough to meet the need. Your head might tell you it is foolish to utter something like that, but when Holy Ghost unction comes upon you, it is not you speaking but the Holy Spirit speaking through you. He is prompting you to speak it out; you taking the liberty to say it is actually the first part of the manifestation of your prayer when you speak it with a believing heart. Jesus' own desires are fulfilled when you abide in Him, when you have such complete intimacy with Him, that you will speak what He wills. You are discerning God's purposes and being a voice for Him.

God delights in delegating His power to men, when He can find people who dare to believe and obey Him. The Lord wants you to speak to the mountains in your life and tell them to drop into the ocean. "Truly I tell you, whoever says to this mountain, Be lifted up and thrown into the sea and does not doubt at all in his heat but believes that what he says will take place, it will be done for him." Mk 11:23 amp He doesn't say, pray, He says say. It is the same thing the Lord told Moses, in effect, "You asked Me to work in these situations, I granted your request and you will have the victory. But I choose to work through you. Speak to the barrier in front of you in My Name and it will obey you." You may not get an immediate response the first time you speak a living word to it, but if you will persist in patient obedience, with an attitude of authority, and a heart full of faith, you WILL see results. Elijah told his servant to go back seven times until he saw a cloud the size of a man's hand. When that cloud showed up, they had to run because of all the rain that was coming. The children of Israel had to march around the walls of Jericho seven times before they could shout those walls down. But the drought did end, the rain did come, the walls did fall and persistence paid off. They determined not to give up even when there seemed to be no hope. It will pay off for you too.

If the devil is decreeing fear, death and destruction against you, you had better get busy combating his thoughts with faith-filled words. God always deals in opposites. If the enemy is predicting gloom and doom, it is time to start dancing and decreeing victory and restoration. The thief once discovered has to restore what he stole sevenfold. Prov. 6:31 Stand firm and do not back down. God will always halt the enemy in his tracks but he needs you as His voice of authority here on earth. David ran at Goliath with his mouth open, "For who is this uncircumcised Philistine that he should defy the armies of the living God?"1 Sam 17: 26b amp

If you allow the devil to throw you a pity party and you attend it by starting to say or think words like, "poor old me, look what I don't have, what I can't do...." You have defeated yourself already. Stand up on your own two feet and throw smart bombs the devil with faith-filled words. Of course you can do all things if you let him give you the strength.

Then there was the woman who wouldn't give up: This persistent Southern lady spoke to her husband's corpse as it lay on the emergency room table, the coroner having signed the death certificate. She laid it on the line and spoke to the lifeless body, speaking to his spirit man. 'The word of the Lord came to you and prophesied that you would go into politics and we would have a son. Now that has not been fulfilled yet, and God is not a man that He should lie. His word quickens the dead and calls those things that be not as though they were.' The body which had been pronounced dead started to stir and come back to life at her words. The spirit of faith in that woman's mouth quickened that corpse, that man rose up and fulfilled his destiny, he became a congressman in the state of Georgia, and their son was born.

When you are in a life or death spiritual battle, you need to be guiding your words with laser-like precision. The hole in the dyke was only stopped by one small boy stopping it with his finger. Being specific with the word is the key. Using a word that brings life to you personally is vital. Make sure you are full of God's word, meditating and muttering it, praying it through. This cannot be you speaking without the spirit of God on it, if you want it to have results. It must be the Lord. If you want it to destroy the works of the enemy you had better have the angel of the Lord as your rear guard. The sons of Sceva thought they could do it on their own and they were blown away when the demon beat them up so badly. They thought they did not need the strength of God and His word. Big mistake. Trying to do it in your own strength only makes a mess. Start delivering your prophetic words in small places, one-on-one, in a Bible study, to whoever the Lord quickens to you. Start to bloom where you are planted, start gleaning like Ruth did in the corners of the field and keep seeking Him. He will take you right into the center of the field where your Kinsman Redeemer is waiting for you.

Job "uselessly opens his mouth and multiplies words without knowledge (drawing the worthless conclusion that the righteous have not more advantage than the wicked,) Job 35:16 amp. Job's mouth is what brought destruction and heartache on him. But he repented in the last chapter, saying "Therefore (I now see) I have (rashly) uttered what I did not understand, things too wonderful for me, which I did not know," Job 42:3b amp. What you say must line up with God's Word. If it is from God's heart it will line up with chapter and verse. Job drew the "worthless conclusion that the righteous have no more advantage than the wicked." If you were to watch the television news long enough you might come to that conclusion too. It is vital what you put in front of your eyes if you want to guarantee what is going to come out of your mouth. Will it be full of faith and power or fear and pity? Fear and pity never healed, saved or helped anyone, but faith and power will knock a home run out of the ballpark every single time.

Chapter 7
"Prayer Of Salvation"

If you have never asked the Lord into your heart, this is your day. These words will change your life for eternity. Just say this prayer out loud, "Dear Lord Jesus, I ask you to come into my life and be my Lord and Savior. Father, Please forgive me of all my sin and cleanse me of all unrighteousness. I thank you Lord, that I am a new creature, and all old things have passed away and behold all things have become new." After you have prayed this prayer, find a good church that teaches the word of God and gets people filled with the Holy Spirit. Get a hold of a Bible, start to read the book of John and ask God to speak to you. He will, and be quick to obey His voice when He does.

TO CONTACT MARY HUDSON:

KEITH HUDSON MINISTRIES
P.O. BOX 50937
IRVINE, CA 92619
(951) 522-8391
arise777@me.com
www.keithhudson.org

Mary has a heart to empower women to rise up in their gifts and callings in Him. She has conducted Arise International crusades nationally and internationally. If you would like to contact her about having one in your area, please email Joel Aragon at bookingthehudsons@gmail.com.

Mary Hudson's Other Ministry Product

- *Contending For Your Miracle* (Audio CD) - $8.00
- *The Joy of the Lord is Your Strength* (Audio CD) - $8.00
- *Contending For the Faith* (Audio CD) - $8.00
- *How Often Does God Talk To You?* (Audio CD) - $8.00
- *Prompted By Faith* (Audio CD) - $8.00